Environmental Lifestyle Guide

For Grade 12 Students

VOL.11 OF 11

Tourism

Jahangir Asadi

Vancouver, BC CANADA

Published by: Silosa Consulting Group Inc.
Vancouver, BC **CANADA**
Email: Info@Silosa.ca
www.silosa.ca

Ordering Information:
Quantity sales. Special discounts are available on quantity purchases by universities, schools, corporations, associations, and others. For details, contact the "Sales Department" at the above mentioned email address.

Environmental lifestyle Guide Vol.11 for Grade.12/J.Asadi —1st ed.
ISBN: 978-1-990451-85-0

Contents

We hope that, 10,000 years from now, future generations will be able to see flowers that provide bees with nectar and pollen and...
BEES provide flowers with the means to reproduce by spreading pollen from flower to flower,....

Jahangir Asadi

This book is dedicated to my professor, Dr.Bijan Esfandiari

Introduction

This book is part of an eleven volume series that is meant to be a standard textbook series, for grades 9 to 12. TTAIN & ESFK & SCG improves quality of life and reduces environmental degradation by fostering new consumption patterns and sustainable lifestyles through International Cooperative Extension Service programs at houses, offices, schools and libraries all over the globe.

Climate change is real. Therefore people have the potential to make a difference now and for future generations. This book provides climate science basics, including the roles that lifestyles and populations play in the climate scenario, the significance of carbon footprints, and an overview of the current climate situation. The manual has been categorized based on humanity's needs starting first with food and ending with tourism. The manual then illustrates the difference between adaptation (taking steps to live with the changes) and mitigation (taking steps to slow the rate of change.)

Adaptation examples include food, energy, transportation, recreation. Mitigation focuses on effectively engaging with local governments, through serving on advisory boards, communicating with public officials, educational institutes, schools, universities, libraries and leading communities towards climate change actions.

One useful way to mitigate climate change is through increasing public knowledge to better understand the impact of the rate of change on plants and animals. This is crucial for preserving species; and for assessing potential insects and disease outbreaks in agriculture, natural resources and public health.

Taking personal action is a key element of this manual.

Citizens are challenged to consume 20% fewer resources, to bring world consumption levels down as much as possible. Readers are given 12 practical steps to take to make the changes. The resources section provides additional information, and readers are encouraged to contact the author for further questions.

As an accessibility action, we have provided Online international courses on climate change control as well. You can access the courses via the following link:

http://TopTenAward.org

SILOSA Consulting Group (SCG)

Silosa Consulting Group (SCG) was established to provide outstanding consulting services of management system & educational standards to individuals, groups, companies, schools, and organizations all over the globe. SCG is publishing an "Environmental Lifestyle Guide " book series as a standard textbook related to increasing environmental awareness of students means being aware of the natural environment and making choices that benefit the earth, rather than hurt it. Vol.1 to 11 (for grades 9 to 12) providing some of the ways to practice environmental awareness include: **Recycling, Conserving energy and water, Reuse, Activism, and others**.

SCG book publishing services and distribution services are connected to over 39,000 booksellers worldwide, including Apple, Amazon, Barnes & Noble, Indigo, Google Play Books, and many more. SCG has enough experiences to help create new and effective environmental educational programmes in different countries all over the world. For more detail, visit our website : http://silosa.ca and/or send your enquirer to the following email:

info@silosa.ca

About ISO 14000 for Students

The International Organization for Standardization is an independent, non-governmental organization, the members of which are the standards organizations of the 165 member countries. It is the world's largest developer of voluntary international standards and it facilitates world trade by providing common standards among nations. More than twenty thousand standards have been set, covering everything from manufactured products and technology to food safety, agriculture, and healthcare.

Kids ISO 14000s
"Kids ISO 14000s" is a new environmental education program for children, based on ISO 14000s, which is international standard for environmental management. Primary aims of this program are: -
1. To teach and train children how to manage the environmental issues (such as energy saving) by themselves through the working book and guide book of this program,
2. To certify those children who showed good accomplishment in the program from highly international authority (as is the case of ISO 14000s)
3. To network those children through the international network (Kids International Network), so that the children can work on the environment, internationally.

2. System of Kids ISO 14000s Program

The system of Kids ISO 14000s Program consists of

1. Operation Headquarter (ArTech).

2. Workbook, Guidebook (originally published by ArTech, and local versions are produced by each countries).

3. Eco-Kids-Instructors for local operation and evaluation of the performance of the children.

4. International accreditation committee for accreditation of accomplishment of the children, for certification of the Eco-Kids-Instructors, as well as overall checks of this program.

5. Linkage with international organizations (such as UNU, UNESCO, etc. …) And also national organizations

More information can be obtained :

www.ISO.org

Canada

Environmental Sustain for Future kids established in Vancouver, BC Canada in 2020. (ESFK) is an international ecolabel focused on taking care of environment for future of kids. ESFK defined as 'self-declared' environmental claims made by manufacturers and businesses based on ISO 14020 series of standards, the claimant can declare the environmental objectives and targets in relation to taking care of environment for future kids. However, this declaration will be verifiable.

Environmental Sustain for Future Kids
Vancouver, BC CANADA

Email: info@esfk.org
Web: www.esfk.org

STEP ELEVEN

All about

'Eco-Tourism'

The term Ecotourism emerged in the late 1980s as a direct result of theworld's acknowledgment and reaction to sustainable practices and global ecological practices. In these instances, the natural-based element of holiday activities together with the increased awareness to minimise the 'antagonistic' impacts of tourism on the environment (which is the boundless consumption of environmental resources) contributed to the demand for ecotourism holidays. This demand was also boosted by concrete evidence that consumers had shifted away from mass tourism towards experiences that were more individualistic and enriching. In addition, these experiences were claimed to be associated with a general search for the natural component during holidays

Definitions of Ecotourism

Ziffer, 1989	'Ecotourism is a form of tourism inspired primarily by the natural history of an area, including its indigenous cultures. The ecotourist visits relatively undeveloped areas in the spirit of appreciation, participation and sensitivity. The ecotourist practices a non-consumptive use of wildlife and natural resources and contributes to the visited area through labor or financial means aimed at directly benefiting the conservation of the site and the economic well-being of the local residents...'
Boo, 1991	'Ecotourism is a nature tourism that contributes to conservation, through generating funds for protected areas, creating employment opportunities for local communities, and offering environmental education.'
Forestry Tasmania, 1994	'Nature-based tourism that is focused on provision of learning opportunities while roviding local and regional benefits, while demonstrating environmental, social, cultural, and economic sustainability'
Richardson, 1993	'Ecologically sustainable tourism in natural areas that interprets local environment and cultures, furthers the tourists' understanding of them, fosters conservation and adds to the well-being of the local people.'
Australia Department of Tourism, 1994	'Nature-based tourism that involves education and interpretation of the natural environment and is managed to be ecologically sustainable. This definition recognizes that natural environment includes cultural components, and that ecologically sustainable involves an appropriate return to the local community and long-term conservation of the resource.'
Figgis, 1993	'Travel to remote or natural areas which aims to enhance understanding and appreciation of natural environment and cultural heritage, avoiding damage or deterioration of the "environment and the experience for others".'
Tickell, 1994	'Travel to enjoy the world's amazing diversity of natural life and human culture without causing damage to either.'

Definitions of Ecotourism (Cont.)

Boyd & Butler, 1993	'A responsible nature travel experience, that contributes to the conservation of the ecosystem while respecting the integrity of host communities and, where possible, ensuring that activities are complementary, or at least compatible, with existing resource- based uses present at the ecosystem.'
Boyd & Butler, 1996	'Ecotourism is a form of tourism which fosters environmental principles, with an emphasis on visiting and observing natural areas'
Goodwin, 1996	'Low impact nature tourism which contributes to the maintenance of species and habitats either directly through a contribution to conservation and/or indirectly by providing revenue to the local community sufficient for local people, and therefore protect, their wildlife heritage area as a source of income.'
Lindberg & McKercher, 1997	'Ecotourism is tourism and recreation that is both nature-based and sustainable.'

Environmental Impacts of Ecotourism

The most proclaimed positive issue is ecotourism's contribution to sustainable resource management through conservation of the natural resources on a direct or indirect basis (Commonwealth of Australia, 1993, 1995; Cater, 1993, 1994; Dearden, 1995)

Environmental impacts	
Direct benefits	Direct costs
• Provides incentive to protect environment, both formally (protected areas) and informally	• Danger that environmental carrying capacities will be unintentionally exceeded, due to:
• Provides incentive for restoration and conversion of modified habitats	• Rapid growth rates Difficulties in identifying, measuring and monitoring impacts over a long period
• Ecotourists actively assisting in habitat enhancement (donations, policing, maintenance, etc.)	• Idea that all tourism induces stress

Environmental impacts (Cont.)	
Indirect benefits	Indirect costs
• Exposure to ecotourism fosters broader commitment to environmental well-being	• Fragile areas may be exposed to less benign forms of tourism (pioneer function)
• Space protected because of ecotourism provide various environmental benefits	• May foster tendencies to put financial value on nature, depending upon attractiveness

Economic Impacts of Ecotourism

The direct and indirect benefits which are derived frombiodiversity conservation, represent the fundamental goal of ecotourism, by attracting visitors to the natural settings and using the revenues to fund conservation and fuel economic development (Commonwealth of Australia, 1995: 12; Cater, 1993, 1994)

Economic impacts	
Direct benefits	Direct costs
• Revenues obtained directly from ecotourists • Creation of direct employment opportunities • Strong potential for linkages with other sectors of the local economy • Stimulation of peripheral rural economies	• Start-up expenses (acquisition of land, establishment of protected areas, superstructure, infrastructure) • Ongoing expenses maintenance of infrastructure, promotion, wages)

Economic impacts (Cont.)	
Indirect benefits	Indirect costs
• Indirect revenues from ecotourists (high multiplier effect) • Tendency of ecotourists to patronise cultural and heritage attractions as 'add-ons' • Economic benefits from sustainable use of protected areas and inherent existence	• Revenue uncertainties to in situ nature if consumption • Revenue leakages due to imports, expatriate or non-local participation, etc. • Opportunity costs • Damage to crops by wildlife

Sociocultural Impacts of Ecotourism

The sustainable component of ecotourism often attests certain direct and indirect sociocultural benefits and costs at the sites and/or at the destination level . Generally speaking, it was proposed that the assessment of the cultural impacts of ecotourism could be based on four criteria , commodification element; culture affecting social change; cultural knowledge; and cultural patrimony elements.

Sociocultural impacts	
Direct benefits	Direct costs
• Ecotourism accessible to a broad spectrum of the population • Aesthetic/spiritual element of experiences • Foster environmental wareness among ecotourists and local population	• Intrusions upon local and possibly isolated cultures • Imposition of elite alien value system • Displacement of local cultures by parks • Erosion of local control (foreign experts, in-migration of job seekers).

Sociocultural impacts (Cont.)	
Indirect benefits	Indirect costs
• Option and existence benefits	• Potential resentment and antagonism of locals • Tourist opposition to aspects of local culture (e.g. hunting, slash-burn agriculture).

Principles of Ecotourism

(1) travel to natural destinations.

(2) minimizes impact. This includes minimizing the impact of development and tourist activity by choosing appropriate building materials, renewable energy sources, visitor management strategies, monitoring techniques and conservation plans.

(3) builds environmental awareness. This includes educational and interpretational material for visitors, educational training for guides and educating the greater public and surrounding community.

(4) provides direct financial benefit for conservation.

(5) provides financial benefits and empowerment for local people. This includes employment of local people, using an all-inclusive stakeholder approach to planning, management and policy development and fostering of partnerships.

(6) respects local culture.

(7) supports human rights.

ONLINE
EDUCATION

START YOUR ONLINE COURSE NOW AFTER YOU HAVE COMPLETED READING THIS BOOK, DO YOUR QUIZZES AND RECEIVE YOUR INTERNATIONAL TRAINING CERTIFICATE OF :

CLIMATE CHANGE CONTROL

JOIN US AT:

WWW.TOPTENAWARD.ORG

KNOWLEDGE TESTS

1) This definition recognizes. that _____ _____ includes cultural components, and that ecologically sustainable involves an appropriate.
A) natural environment
B) environmental labelling
C) Eco tourism
D) All of them
ANSWER:

2) Ecotourism is a form of tourism which fosters environmental principles, with an emphasis on visiting and observing natural areas.
A) True
B) False
ANSWER:

3) 'Ecologically sustainable tourism in natural areas that interprets local environment and cultures, furthers the tourists' understanding of them, fosters conservation and adds to the well-being of the local people.'
A) True
B) False
ANSWER:

4) 'Travel to enjoy the world's amazing diversity of natural life and human culture without causing damage to either.'
A) Goodwin, 1996
B) Richardson,1993
C) Figgis, 1993
D) Tickell, 1994
ANSWER:

5) The direct and indirect benefits which are derived frombiodiversity conservation, represent the fundamental goal of ecotourism, by attracting visitors to the natural settings and using the revenues to fund conservation and fuel economic development
A) True
B) False
ANSWER:

6) The sustainable component of ecotourism often attests certain direct and indirect sociocultural benefits and costs at the sites and/ or at the destination level.
A) True
B) False
ANSWER:

7) Principles of Ecotourism:
A) travel to natural destinations.
B) minimizes impact. This includes minimizing the impact of development and tourist activity by choosing appropriate building materials, renewable energy sources, visitor management strategies, monitoring techniques and conservation plans.
C) builds environmental awareness. This includes educational and interpretational material for visitors, educational training for guides and educating the greater public and surrounding community.
D) All of them
ANSWER:

8) Principles of Ecotourism:
A) provides direct financial benefit for conservation.
B) provides financial benefits and empowerment for local people. This includes employment of local people, using an all-inclusive stakeholder approach to planning, management and policy development and fostering of partnerships.
C) respects local culture
D) All of them
ANSWER:

9) Ecotourism accessible to a broad spectrum of the population
A) True
B) False
ANSWER:

10) Ecotourists actively assisting in habitat enhancement (donations, policing, maintenance, etc.)
A) True
B) False
ANSWER:

Bibliography:

Achama, F. (1995) Defining ecotourism. In L. Haysith and J. Harvey (eds) Nature Conservation and Ecotourism in Central America (pp. 23–32). Florida: Wildlife Conservation Society.

Agardy, M.T. (1993)Accommodating ecotourism in multiple use planning of coastal and marine protected areas. Ocean & Coastal Management 20 (3), 219–239.

Australia Department of Tourism (1994)National Ecotourism Strategy. Canberra: Australia Government Publishing Service.

Ayala, H. (1995) From quality product to eco-product:Will Fiji set a precedent? Tourism Management 16 (1), 39–47.

Barnes, J.L. (1996)Economic characteristics of the demand for wildlife-viewing tourism in Botswana. Development Southern Africa 13 (3), 377–397.

Blamey, R.K. (1995a) The Nature of Ecotourism. Canberra: Bureau of Tourism Research.

Blamey, R.K. (1995b) The elusive market profile: Operationalising ecotourism. Paper presented at the Geography of Sustainable Tourism Conference, University of Canberra, ACT, Australia, September.

Blamey, R.K. (1997) Ecotourism: The search for an operational definition. Journal of Sustainable Tourism 5 (2), 109–130.

Boo, E. (1990) Ecotourism: The Potential and Pitfalls (Vols 1& 2). Washington, DC: World Wide Fund for Nature.

Boo, E. (1991a) Ecotourism: A tool for conservation and development. In J.A. Kusler (compiler) Ecotourism and Resource Conservation: A Collection of Papers (Vol. 1) (pp. 54–60). Madison: Omnipress.

Boo, E. (1991b) Planning for ecotourism. Parks 2 (3), 4–8.

Boo, E. (1992) The Ecotourism Boom: Planning for Development and Management. WHN technical paper series, Paper 2. Washington, DC: WWF.

Boo, E. (1993) Ecotourism planning for protected areas. In K. Lindberg and D.E. Hawkins (eds) Ecotourism: Guide for Planners and Managers (pp. 15–31). North Bennington: The Ecotourism Society.

Bottrill C.G. and Pearce, D.G. (1995) Ecotourism: Towards a key elements to operationalising the concept. Journal of Sustainable Tourism 3 (1), 45–54.

Amberg, N.; Magda, R. Environmental Pollution and Sustainability or the Impact of the Environmentally Conscious Measures of International Cosmetic Companies on Purchasing Organic Cosmetics. Visegrad J. Bioecon. Sustain. Dev. 2018, 1, 23.

Asadi, J., "International Environmental Labelling, Economic Consequencies, Export Magazine, July 2001

Asadi, J. 2008. Mobile Phone as management systems tools, ISO Magazine, Vol.8, No.1

Asadi, J., Eco-Labelling Standards, National Standard Magazine, Sep. 2004.

Barbieux, D.; Padula, A.D. Paths and Challenges of New Technologies: The Case of Nanotechnology-Based Cosmetics Development in Brazil. Adm. Sci. 2018, 8, 16.

Advanced Engineering and Applied Sciences: An International Journal 2014; 4(3): 26-28

Berolzheimer, C. (2006). Pencils: An Environmental Profile.

Chemical Week, 1999. Europe's Beef Ban Tests Precautionary Principle. (August 11).

Chaudri, S.K.; Jain, N.K. History of Cosmetics. Asian J. Pharm. 2009, 7–9, 164–167.

CHOI, J.P. Brand Extension as Informational Leverage. Review of Eco- nomic Studies, Vol. 65 (1998), pp. 655-669.

Conway, G. 2000. Genetically modified crops: risks and promise.

Corrado, M., (1989), The Greening Consumer in Britain, MORI, London

Corrado, M., (1997), Green Behaviour – Sustainable Trends, Sustainable Lives?, MORI, london, accessed via countries. Manila, Asian Development Bank 33p.

Davies, Clive. Chief, Design for the Environment Program, Environmental Protection Agency. Interview. March 24, 2009.

Federal Trade Commission, "Sorting Out Green Advertising Claims." http://www.ftc.gov/bcp/edu/pubs/consumer/general/gen02.shtm (March 26, 2009, March 27, 2009)

Ooyen, Carla. Research Manager with Nutrition Business Journal. Personal correspondence. March 19, 2009.

Tekin, Jenn. Marketing Manager with Packaged Facts & SBI. Personal correspondence. March 17, 2009.

University of California - Berkeley. http://berkeley.edu/news/media/releases/2006/05/22_householdchemicals.shtml (March 26, 2009)

U.S. Department of Health and Human Services, Household Products Database.http://householdproducts.nlm.nih.gov/cgi-bin/household/prodtree?prodcat=Inside+the+Home (March 17,

Women's Voices of the Earth, "Household Cleaning Products and Effects on Human Health."http://www.womenandenvironment.org/campaignsandprograms/SafeCleaning/safecleaninghealth (March 17, 2009)

EMONS, W. Credence Goods Monopolists. International Journal of In- dustrial Organization, Vol. 19 (2001), pp. 375-389.

European Union official website: https://ec.europa.eu/info/about-european-commission/contact_en

Feenstra, R.C. "Exact Hedonic Price Indexes," Review of Economics and Statistics 77 (1995): 634-653.

Feenstra, R.C., and J.A. Levinsohn. "Estimating Markups and Market Conduct with Multidimensional Product Attributes," Review of Economic Studies (62 (1995): 19-52.

ForestEthics. (n.d.). Back to School Report Card.

Forest Stewardship Council: "Principles and criteria for forest stewardship" Document 1.2: <http://www.fscoax.org>

Forsyth, K. 1999. Will consumers pay more for certified wood products? Journal of Forestry 97 (2) : 18-22.

ForestChoice #2 (2014, January 1). ForestChoice #2 Graphite Pencils (12 Pack).

Francois, C., Harris, B. (2014, November 2). How are Mechanical Pencils Made?.

Freeman, A. M III. The Measurement of Environmental and Resource Values. Theory and Methods. Washington D.C.: Resource for the Future, 1993.

Friends of the Earth, 1993. Timber certification and eco-labeling. London, FOE:

Geetha Margret Soundri, "Ecofriendly Antimicrobial Finishing of Textiles Using Natural Extract", Journal of International Academic Research For Multidisciplinary, ISSN: 2320 – 5083, 2014, Vol 2.

Graves, P., J.C. Murdoch, M.A. Thayer, and D. Waldman. "The Robustness of Hedonic Price Estimation: Urban Air Quality," Land Economics 64(1988): 220-233.

Halvorsen, R. and R. Palmquist. "The Interpretation of Dummy Variables in Semilogarithmic Equations." American Economic Review 70:474-75 (1980).

Henderson D. (2008). Opportunity Cost." The Concise Encyclopedia of Economics.

How It's Made. (2009, Nov 17). How It's Made Graphite Pencil Leads [video file].

Imhoff, Dan. "Growing Pains: Organic Cotton Tests the Fibre of Growers and Manufacturers Alike," reprinted on Simple Life's web page (simplelife.com), but first printed by Farmer to Farmer, December 1995.

Incomplete Consumer Information in Laboratory Markets. Journal of Environmental labeling.

ISO 14020, ISO 14021,ISO 14024,ISO 14025, International Organization for Standardization.

Kennedy, P.E. "Estimation with Correctly Interpreted Dummy Variables in Semilogarithmic Equations," American Economic Review 71: 801 (1981).

Kirchho®, S., (2000), Green Business and Blue Angels.

Kraus, Jeff. Lab Technician at the North Carolina School of Textiles.

Labeling Issues, Policies and Practices Worldwide.

Lamport, L. 1998. The cast of (timber) certifiers: who are they? International J. Ecoforestry 11(4): 118-122.

Large Scale impoverishment of Amazonian forests by logging and fire. 1999.

Lathrop, K.W. and Centner, T.J. 1998. Eco-labeling and ISO 14000: An analysis of US regulatory systems and issues concerning adoption of type II standards. Environmental

Lee, J. et al. 1996. Trade related environmental measures; sizing and comparing impacts.

Lehtonen, Markku. 1997. Criteria in Environmental Labeling: A comparative Analysis on Environmental Criteria in Selected Labeling Schemes. Geneva, UNEP. 148p.

LIEBI, T. Trusting Labels: A Matter of Numbers? Working Paper Uni versity of Bern, No. 0201 (2002).

OECD. "Ec-labelling: Actual Effects of Selected Programmes," OCDE/GD (97) 105, 1997, Paris. (available on line at http://www.oecd.org/env/eco/books.htm#trademono)

OECD. 1997a. Case study on eco-labeling schemes. Paris, OECD (30 Dec):

OECD. 1997b. Eco-labeling: Actual Effects of Selected Programs.

Osborne, L. "Market Structure, Hedonic Models, and the Valuation of Environmental Amenities." Unpublished Ph.D. dissertation. North Carolina State University, 1995.

Osborne, L., and V. K. Smith. "Environmental Amenities, Product Differentiation, and market Power," Mimeo, 1997.

Ozanne, L.K. and Vlosky, R.P. 1996. Wood products environmental certification: the United States perspective". Forestry Chronicle 72 (2) : 157-165.

Palmquist, R. B., F. M. Roka, and T.Vukina. "Hog Operations, Environmental Effects, and Residential Property Values," Land Economics 73(1), (1997): 114-24.

Palmquist, R.B. "Hedonic Methods," in J.B Braden and C.D. Kolstad, eds. Measuring the Demand for Environmental Improvement. Amsterdam, NL: Elsevier, 1991.

Paper Mate. (2014). Paper Mate Recycled.

Pento, T. 1997. Implementation of Public Green Procurement Programs (22-31) in Greener Purchasing: Opportunities and Innovations. Sheffield, Greenleaf Publ. 325 p.

Perloff, J. "Industrial Organization Lecture Notes," Mimeo. University of California at Berkeley (1985).

Plant, C. and Plant, J. 1991. Green business: hope or hoax? Philadelphia, New Society Publishers 136 p.

Pencil Making Today (2014, January 1). Pencil Making Today: How to Make a Pencil in 10 Steps.

Polak, J. and Bergholm, K. 1997. Eco-labeling and trade: a cooperative approach (Jan.): Policy in a Green Market. Environmental and Resource Economics 22, 419-

Poore, M.E.D. et al. 1989. No timber without trees. London, Earthscan. 352p.

Raff, D. M.G., and M. Trajtenberg. "Quality-Adjusted Prices for the American Automobile Industry: 1906-1940." NBER Working Paper Series, Working Paper No. 5035, February 1995.

Roberts, J. T. 1998. Emerging global environment standards: prospects and perils. Journal of Developing Societies 14 (1): 144-163.

Rosen, S., "Hedonic Prices and Implicit Markets: Product Differentiation in Pure Competition." Journal of Political Economy. 82: 34-55 (1974).

Ross, B. 1997. Eco-friendly procurement training course for UN HCR. : 126 p.

Sayre, D. 1996. Inside ISO 14000: The competitive advantage of environmental management. Delray Beach FL., St. Lucie Press. 232p.

Suzuki, D. (2014, January 1). PEG Compounds and their contaminants

SHAPIRO, C. Premiums for High Quality Products as Returns to Reputa- tion. Quarterly Journal of Economics, Vol. 98, No. 4 (1983), pp. 659-680.

Stillwell, M. and van Dyke, B. 1999. An activists handbook on genetically modified organisms and the WTO. Washington DC., The Consumer's Choice Council: 20 p.

Semenzato, A.; Costantini, A.; Meloni, M.; Maramaldi, G.; Meneghin, M.; Baratto, G. Formulating O/W Emulsions with Plant-Based Actives: A Stability Challenge for an Eective Product. Cosmetics 2018, 5, 59.

Sources of Plastics (2014, January 1). Sources of Plastics.

Singh, S. (2008, March 6). Paraffin wax.

Saint Jean Carbon. (n.d.). Sri Lankan Graphite.

U.S. Environmental Protection Agency. National Water Quality Fact Inventory: 1990 Report to Congress. EPA 503-9-92-006, Apr. 1992.

UK Eco-labelling Board website, accessed via http://www.ccosite.co.uk/Ecolabel-UK/

US Environmental Protection Agency (EPA742-R-99-001): 40 p. <www.epa.gov/opptintr/epp>

US EPA, 1993. Determinants of effectiveness for environmental certification and labeling programs. Washington, D.C., US Environmental Protect

US EPA, 1993. Status report on the use of environmental labels worldwide. Washington, D.C., US Environmental Protection Agency (742-R-93-001 September).

US EPA, 1993. The use of life-cycle assessment in environmental labeling. Washington, D.C., US Environmental Protection Agency (742-R-93-003 September).

US EPA, 1998. Environmental labeling: issues, policies, and practices worldwide. Washington DC., Environmental Protection Agency, Pollution Prevention Division Prepared by Abt

USG, 1998. Greening the government through waste prevention, recycling, and federal acquisition. Washington, D.C., Executive Order 13101 (September).

Kijjoa, A.; Sawangwong, P. Drugs and Cosmetics from the Sea. Mar. Drugs 2004, 2, 73–82. [CrossRef]

Wang, J.; Pan, L.; Wu, S.; Lu, L.; Xu, Y.; Zhu, Y.; Guo, M.; Zhuang, S. Recent Advances on Endocrine Disrupting Eects of UV Filters. Int. J. Environ. Res. Public Health 2016, 13, 782.

Bilal, A.I.; Tilahun, Z.; Shimels, T.; Gelan, Y.B.; Osman, E.D. Cosmetics Utilization Practice in Jigjiga Town, Eastern Ethiopia: A Community Based Cross-Sectional Study. Cosmetics 2016, 3, 40.

Ting, C.T.; Hsieh, C.M.; Chang, H.-P.; Chen, H.-S. Environmental Consciousness and Green Customer Behavior: The Moderating Roles of Incentive Mechanisms. Sustainability 2019, 11, 819.

Chen, K.; Deng, T. Research on the Green Purchase Intentions from the Perspective of Product Knowledge. Sustainability 2016, 8, 943.

Wang, H.; Ma, B.; Bai, R. How Does Green Product Knowledge Eectively Promote Green Purchase Intention? Sustainability 2019, 11, 1193.

Nguyen, T.T.H.; Yang, Z.; Nguyen, N.; Johnson, L.W.; Cao, T.K. Greenwash and Green Purchase Intention: The Mediating Role of Green Skepticism. Sustainability 2019, 11, 2653.

Cinelli, P.; Coltelli, M.B.; Signori, F.; Morganti, P.; Lazzeri, A. Cosmetic Packaging to Save the Environment: Future Perspectives. Cosmetics 2019, 6, 26.

Eixarch, H.; Wyness, L.; Siband, M. The Regulation of Personalized Cosmetics in the EU. Cosmetics 2019, 6, 29.

CANADA SILVER BEAVER BADGE

Participate in our Online Classes to earn these exclusive digital badges!
www.toptenaward.org

Design & Development by:

Tara Asadi

CANADA BRONZE BEAVER BADGE

Participate in our Online Classes to earn these exclusive digital badges!
www.toptenaward.org

Design & Development by:

Tara Asadi

CANADA GOLD BEAVER BADGE

Participate in our Online Classes to earn these exclusive digital badges!

Design & Development by:

Tara Asadi

Environmental Lifestyle Guide

For Grade 9

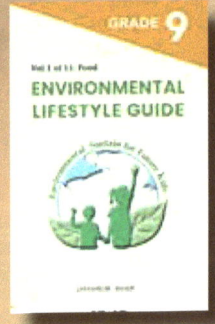

For Grade 10

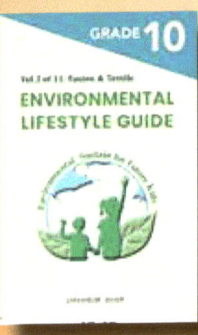

Plus Online Certification Tests via:
https://toptenaward.org

Standard Text Books

For Grade 11

For Grade 12

 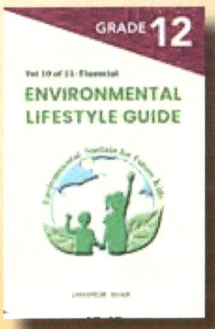 

**Environmental Lifestyle Guide
Standard Text Book**
For Students Grade 9 to 12
Available in more than
39,000 Bookstores
all over the globe.
https://ecofriendlyeducation.com

Cooperation by:
Top Ten Award International Network
&
Environmental Sustain for Future Kids

www.ingramcontent.com/pod-product-compliance
Lightning Source LLC
Chambersburg PA
CBHW040900120626

46551CB00001B/101